W9-AVJ-348

Raising Student Aspirations

Classroom Activities
for Grades 6-8

Russell J. Quaglia and Kristine M. Fox

CONFIDENCE to TAKE ACTION

LEADERSHIP and RESPONSIBILITY

SPIRIT of ADVENTURE

CURIOSITY and CREATIVITY

FUN and EXCITEMENT

SENSE of ACCOMPLISHMENT

HEROES

BELONGING

Research Press 2612 North Mattis Avenue • Champaign, Illinois 61822 • [800] 519-2707 • www.researchpress.com

Composition by Jeff Helgesen
Cover design by Linda Brown, Positive I.D. Graphic Design, Inc.
Printed by McNaughton & Gunn, Inc.

ISBN 0-87822-481-5
Library of Congress Catalog Number 2002095759

Contents

Chapter 4: Fun and Excitement

Chapter 5: Curiosity and Creativity

Chapter 6: Spirit of Adventure

Chapter 7: Leadership and Responsibility

Chapter 8: Confidence to Take Action

Foreword

Russ Quaglia is an educator with an unusual mission. He wants children not only to be successful in school but to have fun doing it. As the founder and director of the Global Institute for Student Aspirations, he has earned a wide and enviable reputation as a champion of student motivation.

In numerous books, articles, presentations, and TV appearances, Russ has laid out his deceptively simple formula for getting middle school children to achieve their full potential. It is a formula based on solid research and shaped by eight interrelated conditions: Belonging, Heroes, Sense of Accomplishment, Fun and Excitement, Curiosity and Creativity, Spirit of Adventure, Leadership and Responsibility, and Confidence to Take Action.

You will find each of these conditions highlighted in this book. Russ and co-author Kristine Fox have provided middle school classroom teachers with a rich variety of activities designed to lay a foundation for student aspirations, and then provide the motivation to make aspirations a way of life.

Although it's a book that was written specifically for teachers, there is rich food for thought here for school administrators. Speaking for myself and the 29,500 members of the National Association of Elementary School Principals (NAESP), I see a seamless blending of Russ Quaglia's approach to building student aspirations and the creation of a school culture that embraces the whole child.

The principal's role as an instructional leader is not only to strive for success for all students, but to inspire them and make them feel part of a learning community. Principals accomplish this by training and encouraging teachers to imbue in their students the very qualities that Russ has consistently championed.

Look over the activities in this book and you will see why Russ's approach has been so successful. What child wouldn't have fun helping make a class quilt, playing word games, learning how to juggle, decorating the classroom, or making a secret code? They are all here, and each has a specific objective to Russ's mission to mold lifelong aspirations into the character of our students.

American education needs more visionaries like Russ Quaglia.

Vincent L. Ferrandino
Executive Director
National Association
    of Elementary School Principals

Introduction

As a teacher, you have the opportunity to create wonderful learning environments for your students every day. You have the power to make school an exciting, creative, and engaging place where students want to learn. Schools that support, understand, and truly believe in the potential of all students are on their way to developing a culture that supports student aspirations. Promoting student aspirations means that, as a teacher, you are inspiring your students to reach their full potential.

We have identified eight conditions that need to be in place in order for aspirations to flourish. These conditions are fostered through classroom activities, interactions, discussions, and school-wide initiatives. The eight conditions are as follows:

1. Belonging
2. Heroes
3. Sense of Accomplishment
4. Fun and Excitement
5. Curiosity and Creativity
6. Spirit of Adventure
7. Leadership and Responsibility
8. Confidence to Take Action

The activities in this book are designed to help you understand and promote these eight conditions. Although the conditions are described and meant to be introduced in your classroom in a set order, they also fit into three distinct categories.

Three Conditions That Serve as the Foundation for Raising Student Aspirations

The first condition is *belonging*. Belonging activities focus on helping students feel valued for their unique talents and interests. At the same time, these activities help to establish a community in your classroom. You should focus on establishing the condition of belonging the minute students enter the building on the first day of school. You should then continually support and reinforce this condition throughout the school year.

The second condition, *heroes,* focuses on helping students find at least one adult they can trust and turn to for advice. This adult serves as a hero by connecting with the student and promoting the student's desire to connect with others as well. Hero activities help students discover who the real heroes are in their lives, as well as understand that they, too, are heroes. Students who have high aspirations also have real heroes in their lives—people they can turn to for advice, support, and guidance.

The third condition, *sense of accomplishment,* promotes effort, perseverance, and good citizenship. Although academic achievement is critically important to students, there is more to learning than making the grade. Sense of accomplishment activities encourage students to put forth effort and persevere so that they will be successful in life as they mature into responsible citizens.

Three Conditions That Motivate Students and Instill Enthusiasm in the Classroom

The fourth condition is *fun and excitement.* Like the next two conditions, it focuses on the importance of making learning engaging for all students. Fun and excitement activities concentrate on helping students to enjoy school by teaching them to laugh while they learn. You will notice that students who find school exciting will also be engaged and interested in the learning process. They will feel motivated and enthusiastic about what you are teaching them.

The fifth condition, *curiosity and creativity,* is notable not only because it allows students to question and explore what they are learning, but also because it encourages them to remain inquisitive both inside and outside the classroom.

The sixth condition, *spirit of adventure,* has to do with your supporting students to take healthy risks, set goals for themselves, and not worry about failing. Activities that promote spirit of adventure encourage students to set high, achievable goals. Although students may fail in their first few attempts to take healthy risks and set meaningful goals, they can—with your help—learn to keep trying. By persevering, they will have captured the essence of the condition of spirit of adventure.

Two Conditions That Establish the Mind-Set Students Need in Order to Aspire

The seventh condition, *leadership and responsibility,* involves giving every student a voice in the learning environment. Leadership and responsibility activities teach students to be leaders and to work with others. All students have the potential to be leaders and to cooperate with those around them. What they need from you is your desire to teach them the necessary skills and to support them as they develop their unique leadership styles. With your help, they will acquire the mind-set they need in order to aspire.

The eighth condition, *confidence to take action,* relies on your encouraging students to believe in themselves and their abilities. Activities that promote confidence to take action support the development of your students' self-image and also acknowledge their special talents and wonderful contributions to your class, your school, and the world at large.

How the Eight Conditions Benefit Everyone

Supporting student aspirations in the classroom is both exciting and rewarding. As a teacher, you need to understand that promoting aspirations is not the same as implementing an add-on unit or a special program; rather, it is a way of thinking. Fostering aspirations in the classroom is about believing that all students deserve to be acknowledged, understood, cared about, and supported in all their wonderful endeavors.

The activities presented in this book are meant to enhance what great teachers do every day. Great teachers engage their students, have a passion for teaching and learning, and truly love the teaching profession. Keep in mind that these activities should be used to complement a school culture that already promotes and supports the development of student aspirations. It is hoped that these activities will help students and staff better understand the eight conditions that affect the development of their own aspirations.

The introduction of these activities in the classroom is a great way to begin raising student aspirations. Ideally, you, the teacher, should participate in these activities, too. Most of the activities can be done at any point in the school year, can be adapted for a variety of grade levels, and can be modified to suit the unique nature of your classroom.

We are well aware of the constant time pressures teachers face every day. We also know that investing time and energy in promoting student aspirations will have a positive effect on you, your students, and everyone in your school. These activities will breathe new life into your classroom and create an exciting learning environment. We hope you have fun with them as you help student aspirations flourish.

CHAPTER ONE

BELONGING

CONFIDENCE to TAKE ACTION

LEADERSHIP and RESPONSIBILITY

SPIRIT of ADVENTURE

CURIOSITY and CREATIVITY

FUN and EXCITEMENT

SENSE of ACCOMPLISHMENT

HEROES

BELONGING

ACTIVITY 1   A Thousand Words

A familiar saying is that a picture is worth a thousand words. Pictures representing the condition of belonging can be quite powerful. This activity encourages students to be creative and at the same time helps them search for what belonging means to them as individuals.

Materials
- ► Magazines
- ► Optional: cameras, photo album
- ► Scissors and glue
- ► Writing paper and pencils or pens

Instructions
1. Assign students the task of either cutting out pictures from magazines or taking photos that represent to them the condition of belonging.
2. Have students create a collage, a photo album, or anything else that displays their pictures and photos.
3. Ask your students to explain in writing how these pictures and photos represent belonging.
4. Allow time for students to share and discuss their work with the class.

Discussion
1. In what ways do you see students belonging at school?
2. Why do some students not seem to belong anywhere?
3. How could our school enhance the condition of belonging for students?

Enrichment
Ask students to interview classmates and gather their ideas on belonging. What does it mean to them, for example, to belong to a group or a club?

ACTIVITY 2   Welcome to Our School

Most schools hold events for parents, community members, and students throughout the school year. These events are especially beneficial in that they engender in the students a sense of pride in their school. This activity gives students the opportunity to show off their school, to serve as goodwill ambassadors.

Materials

▶ Writing paper and pencils or pens

Instructions

1. Tell your students they are going to help welcome visitors to the school whenever these guests arrive for special events.

2. Pair up students and ask them to think about how they should properly welcome someone.

3. Try a practice run in which teachers enter the building and students greet them and answer questions these "visitors" may have.

4. Prepare a schedule so students will know when it's their turn to be a goodwill ambassador for the school.

Discussion

1. How can we make community members feel welcome in our school?

2. How can the community be more welcoming to the students?

3. How did you feel about being a goodwill ambassador?

Enrichment

Ask students to create a survey for the visitors they escort around the building. The survey should relate to belonging and how the school can be more welcoming for adults and students.

ACTIVITY 3　　Our Class

Establishing the condition of belonging begins in the classroom. Students should feel that their classroom belongs to them and is unique to them. For this feeling to exist, students need to have input into how the class looks and runs. This activity allows students to personalize their classroom.

Materials
▶ Optional: paint and paintbrushes

▶ Optional: writing paper and pencils or pens

Instructions
1. Decide how you will allow students to personalize the classroom. Some suggestions follow: painting a mural, rearranging the room, creating class rules and procedures, even helping teach a lesson now and then.

2. Be sure to emphasize to the students that this is their classroom and that their input in the activity you have chosen is vital.

3. Give students sufficient time to plan and implement their activity.

4. Revisit this activity throughout the school year.

Discussion
1. Why is it important that this classroom be yours?

2. How can we increase the feeling of belonging at our school?

3. How do we show respect for our school?

Enrichment
Solicit student input and ideas for lesson development. Give students the opportunity to co-teach and help develop tests.

ACTIVITY 4   Trust Me

One important component of belonging is trust. Students need to trust each other and their teacher before they can feel comfortable talking with each other; however, trust takes time and patience to develop. This activity represents one small step toward creating a classroom of trust by having partners rely on each other.

Materials
- ▶ Examples of Trust Me Cards (Create enough additional cards for your class.)
- ▶ Pencils or pens

Instructions
1. Have students pair up.
2. Select one student in the pair to be the leader; have the other be the follower.
3. Give the leader of each pair of students a card bearing a Trust Me example.
4. Have the leader read the directions for the activity to the follower. Make sure the follower performs the prescribed task while keeping his or her eyes shut.
5. Repeat the activity, having the leader and follower switch roles and making sure the pair are given a brand-new Trust Me example to play out.
6. Remind students to be careful during this activity. The leader should be responsible for the safety of the follower.

Discussion
1. What is it like having to trust someone?
2. What needs to be in place for us to trust each other?
3. How does it feel to be responsible for someone else's safety?

Enrichment
With your students, explore what it would be like not to have your eyesight. What would it feel like to be different from so many people? How would you rely on other people to help you?

Examples of Trust Me Cards

1. **Starting at the back of the classroom, walk backward toward the front as I keep you out of harm's way.**

2. **Sit at your desk and, using the paper and pencil I've provided for you, draw a scene in which you are taking part in a favorite activity. I will be there to help you keep pencil to paper.**

3. **Do 10 jumping jacks. I will make sure you don't bump into anyone.**

4. **Sit down in a chair, stand up, walk to another chair, and sit down again. Do this 10 times. I will be there to keep you from falling down.**

ACTIVITY 5　　Outsiders

Reading people's stories about their struggles with acceptance can be a powerful teaching tool for students. There are many inspiring stories about people who struggle to fit in on a daily basis or people who, in spite of being outsiders, defy their stereotypes and do wonderful things with their lives.

Materials
- ▶ Stories about people who are considered outsiders
- ▶ Optional: poetry or musical lyrics that focus on the same "outsider" theme

Instructions
1. Provide students with a selection of stories they can read about outsiders.
2. Allow students a specified amount of time to read their stories.
3. Ask students to write about the stories they've read and also about a time when they themselves experienced being on the outside.
4. Give students the option of sharing their work with the rest of the class.

Discussion
1. How were the characters in your story deemed outsiders?
2. How do you see students in our school acting like outsiders?
3. What does it feel like to be an outsider?

Enrichment
Give students the opportunity to interview adults in the community and to ask them what it's like being an outsider. (Students are often surprised to learn that even prominent and powerful people have felt like outsiders at certain times in their lives.)

ACTIVITY 6   The Square

Working together as a class is a great way to develop a sense of belonging. There are a variety of ways to have your students work together. You may choose group projects or assignments or just be creative with your seating arrangement. This activity is a fun way for students to problem solve together.

Materials

▶ A 4 × 4–foot section of tarpaulin or other flexible material, such as cardboard

Instructions

1. Divide the class into groups of six and give each group a tarp.

2. Have the students stand on their tarp.

3. Challenge the students to jump up and flip the tarp over without stepping on the ground, reminding them to be safe as they perform the activity.

4. Explain to the students that it will take teamwork, practice, and good communication for them to be successful with this activity.

Discussion

1. What was the biggest barrier you faced in accomplishing this activity?

2. How did you overcome this barrier?

3. How important is teamwork? Why?

Enrichment

Give the students a group challenge on a weekly basis. The activity should involve a problem that must be worked out through discussion and teamwork.

ACTIVITY 7   Laughter

There are few things that bring a group together quite as quickly as laughter. Students and adults who share lighthearted moments are likely to seek further opportunities to get together and become better acquainted.

Materials

► Writing paper and pencils or pens

Instructions

1. Write the following statement on the chalkboard: "A smile is the one universal language."
2. Ask your students what they think about this statement.
3. After you have given them time to think about the statement, have the students write about a funny experience they once had. Make sure you also share a funny experience of your own with the class.
4. Throughout the week, give the students a chance to share their stories with everyone else.

Discussion

1. Why does it feel so good to laugh?
2. How many times a day do you laugh?
3. How can we make our class more fun, yet still learn?

Enrichment

Ask students to research the topic of laughter. Some students may want to explore what happens physiologically when someone laughs, whereas others may prefer to discuss famous humorists or comedians.

ACTIVITY 8   Our Assets

No matter what class you teach, your students possess many talents and assets. Although some students have talents that are obvious, others often are never given the opportunity to shine. In order to maintain one's individuality and still be part of a group, the group must be aware of the skills one brings to the group. This activity should help the class understand the concept.

Materials
- List of Assets
- Pencils or pens

Instructions

1. Give your students the List of Assets.
2. Ask them to circle three assets they bring to the group.
3. Read aloud each asset on the list. As you do, ask the students to raise their hands if they chose that asset as one of their three. Write one student's name on the chalkboard for every asset you mention.
4. After all the assets have been assigned, let the students know they are going to be responsible for showing the class that they do indeed possess the asset they said they possess. If there are any assets on your list that no one has claimed credit for, see if any of your students are willing to try to develop these assets.
5. Discuss with your students how it is possible that, as individuals, we may be missing some assets, but as a group, we still have a lot to offer.

Discussion

1. What other assets should we add to our list?
2. What asset would you most like to develop?
3. How do we develop assets?

Enrichment

Give your students the opportunity to take a personality or learning inventory. Students often are fascinated to learn how important their skills and talents are to their learning.

List of Assets

Cooperative	Motivated
Good writer	Forgiving
Good citizen	Empathic
Polite	Unprejudiced
Respectful	Supportive
Sympathetic	Trustworthy
Resourceful	Avid reader
Creative	Hardworking
Pleasant	Honest
Capable of leadership	Persevering

Raising Student Aspirations: Classroom Activities for Grades 6–8
© 2003 by Russell J. Quaglia and Kristine M. Fox. Champaign, IL: Research Press (800) 519-2707

Challenge Activities for Belonging

For Students
- ▶ For one week, have students eat lunch with classmates they normally do not eat with. Have them take the time to really get to know someone they usually do not hang out with.
- ▶ Instruct students to give a second chance to someone they really do not like. Suggest that students who are not friends (or friendly with each other) work together on a project or assignment.
- ▶ Have students spread "positive rumors" about their classmates.

For Teachers
- ▶ Learn something new about one of your students each day. Use this knowledge during class or casual interaction with the student.
- ▶ Hang out in the hallway between classes or when students are entering or exiting the building. Say hello to them and make yourself accessible for casual conversation. Encourage your colleagues to do the same.
- ▶ Maintain a positive attitude when in the teachers' lunchroom. Don't allow negative student or teacher gossip.

CHAPTER TWO

HEROES

CONFIDENCE to TAKE ACTION

LEADERSHIP and RESPONSIBILITY

SPIRIT of ADVENTURE

CURIOSITY and CREATIVITY

FUN and EXCITEMENT

SENSE of ACCOMPLISHMENT

HEROES

BELONGING

ACTIVITY 1   **Our Heroes**

Heroes live in communities all across the country. They may be people who served in time of war, who volunteer at the local hospital, or who simply take the time to be nice to the neighborhood kids.

Materials

▶ Videotaping equipment

Instructions

1. Inform your class that they are going to make a movie about the heroes in their community. To help them get started, do the following:

   Encourage your students to broaden their definition of heroes.

   Help them brainstorm all the different people who may be heroes.

   Remind them not to limit their image of heroes to adults; there may be some students who are heroes.

2. Set up a division of labor, assigning students jobs such as researchers, interviewers, videographers, and so on.

3. After the students decide on their subjects, send a crew of students to interview and film the local heroes.

4. Once the production is completed, have your students show the video to other classes in the school. You may even want to show the film at a meeting of the school board or at other community events.

Discussion

1. What traits did the heroes have in common?
2. What surprised you about any of the local heroes?
3. How else can we publicize the good deeds performed by the heroes in our community?

Enrichment

Have your students create individual hero books about the local people they highlighted. These books can be given to students in the younger grades to read.

Throughout the year, create new hero books as needed.

Students often forget that they can be heroes, too. Some already are. For example, younger students look up to older students for advice and guidance and also because they think the older students are "cool." Their attitude sets the stage for older students who get a chance to serve as mentors. Although it takes time and a real commitment to be a mentor, the rewards are well worth the effort. Keep in mind that there should be an adult on hand who is willing to guide and train the older students to be mentors to the younger students.

Materials
► Mentoring Scenarios
► Writing paper and pencils or pens

Instructions
1. Discuss with your class the idea of mentoring younger students.
2. Give the students the Mentoring Scenarios to help prepare them to be mentors. Have them jot down their answers on a separate sheet of paper so they can refer to them during a class discussion.
3. Brainstorm with the students different activities to do with younger kids. Remind your students that recess and lunch are opportune times to get together with these children.
4. Tell your students that mentoring may involve a task as simple as reading with the same few students every week.
5. Pair up two older students with two younger students and let the magic begin.

Discussion
1. What surprised you about working with younger students?
2. How are kids today different than they were when you were in that grade?
3. What do you have to offer the younger students?

Enrichment
Have your students plan and host an after-school game day for younger kids. Students will have to hold several meetings and planning sessions with the administration. They may also have to raise money to buy supplies.

Mentoring Scenarios

Write your responses to the following scenarios on a separate sheet of paper (numbered 1 through 8) and prepare to discuss them with the rest of the class.

1. The student you are working with is very quiet. She never wants to talk.

   What would you do?

2. You notice that the student you are working with is very aggressive with other students on the playground.

   What would you do?

3. Your teacher has told you that the student you are mentoring never has her homework done.

   What would you do?

4. The student you are working with says he does not have any friends and that no one likes him.

   What would you do?

5. The family of the student you are working with is moving away in a few weeks. She is very sad.

   What would you do?

6. The student you are working with wants to meet with you every day. However, you are allowed to meet only once a week; otherwise, you will miss too much class time.

   What would you do?

7. You notice that other students have been making fun of the student you are mentoring.

   What would you do?

8. Every time you meet with your student, you do the same things. It is becoming rather boring.

   What would you do?

ACTIVITY 3   It's All in the Bag

Recognizing your own positive traits is an important step in becoming a hero. Students who know their strengths are better able to use them to help others. It is also important for classmates to know each other's strengths. In this activity, each student is going to create his or her own bag of personal attributes.

Materials
- ► Lunch bags or paper sacks
- ► 5 slips of paper per student and pencils or pens
- ► Tape

Instructions
1. Give each student five slips of paper.
2. Instruct your students to write down one positive trait of theirs per slip of paper and then put the slips in the bag.
3. Ask students to pull one or two traits from their bag and share them with the class.
4. Stack all the class's traits in one big pile.
5. Use tape to post the traits on the walls of the classroom. (If more than one class occupies the room, tape the traits to a large sheet of paper that can be rolled up and brought out periodically.)

Discussion
1. What traits surprised you?
2. Are we missing any positive traits as a group? (To help the students with this question, think of a few missing positive traits ahead of time.)
3. How can we develop some of our missing traits?

Enrichment
Allow time for your students to write about their personal traits. How do these traits manifest themselves?

Create a plan of action for each student to develop one new trait.

What's Inside?

It's no secret that we often judge people by appearances or by the titles they hold. Children and adults alike frequently regard as their heroes people they do not know personally; these people are heroes because they are rich and famous, talented athletes and actors—not because they have personally helped those who consider them heroes.

Materials
- ▶ 4 different items that can fit inside a gift box
- ▶ 4 gift boxes and an assortment of gift wrap
- ▶ Slips of paper and pencils or pens
- ▶ Tape and a marker

Instructions
1. Assemble four very different items, such as a new toy car, a pencil, a book, and a pack of gum.
2. Put each item in a gift box and wrap each box differently. (The idea is to make the nicest gift appear shabby and the worst gift appear attractive by wrapping them accordingly.)
3. Mark the boxes 1, 2, 3, and 4 and line them up in front of the class.
4. Give students a slip of paper and ask them to number the paper from 1 to 4.
5. Tell the students what items you have wrapped and ask them to guess what is in each box.
6. After all the students have answered, have them share their guesses.
7. Unwrap the packages so the students can see how successful they were at guessing the contents.

Discussion
1. How do we tend to judge people the way we judged the boxes?
2. Why did you think something nice was in the best-looking box?
3. Share a time when you saw someone being judged unfairly.

Enrichment
Continue the discussion during the next class period. The concepts of prejudice and judging another by outside appearances can be explored in many ways. Research historical figures who have faced prejudice, or take the time to talk about how students in the school are judged unfairly. How do we move beyond quick and often harmful first impressions?

Although we adults understand how important it is for young people to get to know older people, we must acknowledge that the reverse also holds true. This activity can help break down many barriers and actually create a more caring community in which people from different generations get to know each other.

Materials ▶ Writing paper and pencils or pens

Instructions

1. Ask your students to write their life stories. If you wish, you may also have them produce a play, a video, or anything else, as long as it represents their life up to this point. Have them end their stories with thoughts about what the future holds for them.

2. Once the students have finished their stories, invite people from the community into the classroom to hear what the students have to tell about their lives.

3. Encourage your students to visit nursing homes or assisted living centers, where they can share their stories with people from earlier generations.

Discussion

1. What did you learn about yourself during this project?

2. What would you like to add to your life story during the next 10 years?

3. What would you like to add to your life story before you graduate from high school?

Enrichment   Although this task may involve numerous interviews and quite a bit of legwork, ask the students to write the life story of a parent or another relative. Compile these life stories into a book.

ACTIVITY 6   Famous Quotes

Thinking about inspirational quotes is a great way for students to start their day. Undoubtedly, many of their heroes have been quoted as saying things that are well worth repeating. This activity will give your students many famous quotes to ponder.

Materials
- ▶ Loose-leaf writing paper and pencils or pens
- ▶ A loose-leaf notebook

Instructions
1. Tell your students that they are going to help develop a book of quotes.
2. Ask each student to gather 10 quotes that are significant to them and write them down. (Make sure the class has access to library materials so that they can search for famous quotes from their heroes.)
3. Have the students share several of their quotes with the class and explain why the quotes are meaningful to them.
4. Collect all the quotes and place them in a notebook. You and your students may also want to post some of the quotes on the walls of the classroom.
5. Share a quote with the class every day.

Discussion
1. What makes a quote famous?
2. What is your all-time favorite quote or saying? Why?
3. What are some famous quotes that you do not understand?

Enrichment
Invite students to select their favorite quotes and use them as mottoes.

Encourage students to create their own mottoes.

Allow students to design their own "business" cards, complete with their favorite mottoes.

What's in the News?

Heroes are highlighted in the news every day. Although the local paper may highlight someone who recently performed an act of kindness, the national media will, of necessity, focus on more universally known heroes. Because most students do not take the time to read the paper in the morning, having them search for articles about heroes is a great way to promote their reading of the news.

Materials
► Local and national newspapers and magazines
► Various Internet sites

Instructions
1. Every week, have two students search newspapers and magazines and the Internet for stories about heroes.
2. Encourage them to find three or four unique and interesting stories.
3. At the end of the week, have the two students share their findings.
4. Inject even more interest in the activity by sharing with your students your own exciting hero stories.

Discussion
1. What traits do our heroes have in common?
2. What heroic deed have you done?
3. Do you know anyone who should be recognized as a hero?

Enrichment
Ask your students to come up with hero stories that have yet to be written. For example, you may have them write about a businessperson who helped pay for a new playground or about a person who works in a homeless shelter.

Have students work together in small groups, write hero stories, and submit them to the local newspaper for publication.

Compile the stories your students have written and share them with other classes.

ACTIVITY 8   Create a Hero

Students often have different ideas about what a hero is or is not. It is therefore important for everyone in the class to understand what makes a person a hero. This activity allows students to create a hero with tangible, realistic traits.

Materials
- ▶ Extra-large sheets of butcher or drawing paper
- ▶ Markers

Instructions

1. Allow your students to work in pairs.

2. Let students know that they are going to create and draw new heroes who possess tangible, realistic traits. These heroes are not like Superman or Superwoman; they can't fly, nor do they have X-ray vision. They do, however, possess qualities such as bravery, honesty, and perseverance.

3. Have the students draw their heroes on the butcher or drawing paper.

4. Tell the students that each hero is allowed only five special traits. The students are to write these traits inside the outline of the hero's body.

5. Ask students to explain why these traits are important.

6. Have the students name their heroes and present them to the class.

Discussion

1. What single heroic trait would you like to possess?

2. What do you think is your strongest heroic trait?

3. Why is it important for us to be heroes to others?

Enrichment

Ask students to think of ways they can be better heroes at school. The class should brainstorm as many ideas as they can think of. Next, ask each student to choose one heroic trait or activity to work on. The class should review their progress every week.

Challenge Activities for Heroes

For Students
- ▶ Encourage students to join a community mentoring program. Urge each student to be a mentor or a friend to a younger student or an older person in your community.
- ▶ Have students write notes to people they know who have made a difference in their lives. Have them take the time to appreciate their everyday heroes.
- ▶ Tell students to take the time to get to know one of their classmates. Have them help a classmate with homework or by studying for a test together.

For Teachers
- ▶ Develop a teacher mentoring program at your school for new and veteran teachers.
- ▶ Write a note of appreciation to someone who has been your professional hero—someone who believes in you and encourages you to be the best you can be.
- ▶ Take the time to be a hero to a child every day. Say hello and ask your students how they are doing. Attend an extracurricular activity or chat after lunch with a few students.
- ▶ Send notes to former students who have already graduated, asking how they are doing and wishing them all the best.

CHAPTER THREE

SENSE of ACCOMPLISHMENT

CONFIDENCE to TAKE ACTION

LEADERSHIP and RESPONSIBILITY

SPIRIT of ADVENTURE

CURIOSITY and CREATIVITY

FUN and EXCITEMENT

SENSE of ACCOMPLISHMENT

HEROES

BELONGING

ACTIVITY 1   National Anthems

Perhaps one of the most moving ways that countries convey their pride of citizenship is through their national anthems. Through song, an anthem tells a story that is meaningful to the citizens of that country. This activity encourages students to explore the history and meaning of other countries' national anthems.

Materials
- A CD player and a CD of the U.S. national anthem
- Books and magazines about, and also from, other countries

Instructions
1. Begin this activity by playing the U.S. national anthem.
2. Ask students to think about the anthem's words and what they mean.
3. After a brief discussion, share the history of the anthem with your students.
4. Invite students to choose a country that interests them. Have them explore the country's anthem and research the origins of the anthem so they have a good idea as to why the particular song was chosen.
5. Give students enough time to share with the class the anthems they chose to explore and the information they uncovered about the countries they decided to study.

Discussion
1. What do you like about our national anthem?
2. Do you think a different song would be better or more appropriate? Why?
3. Why do countries have anthems, flags, and other national symbols?

Enrichment
Have your students explore the design of the U.S. flag and other national symbols, as well as anything else that may be unique to the United States. For instance, what customs are unique to our country? How is our diet different from that of other countries? What types of entertainment that we like distinguish us from those countries? How does our way of life support good citizenship?

Most people who have accomplished great things have, at one time or another, experienced failure along the way. Scientists who find cures for diseases devote many years to their charge. Great athletes must put forth incredible effort; still, they often fail to achieve their goals. Students need to realize that everyone fails, but the ones who succeed are willing to brush off failure and persevere.

Materials
- ▶ Thomas Edison Story
- ▶ Pencils or pens

Instructions
1. Give students the Thomas Edison Story, which is followed by space for students to write My Own Success Story.
2. After they have read the Thomas Edison Story, have them discuss their impressions of it.
3. Ask students to think about their own lives and then write My Own Success Story, complete with setbacks or failures they encountered. (You, too, should share a story about yourself that tells about a failure that turned into a success.)
4. End the discussion by asking students how they can turn a failure into a success or, at the least, a learning experience.

Discussion
1. What are some failures that you think people have faced throughout history?
2. Some people are afraid to succeed. What does this mean?
3. If you were giving advice to a younger student regarding success, what would your advice be?

Enrichment
Ask students to interview their parents about their greatest successes in life. What did it take for them to succeed? What obstacles did they face? Did they ever feel that they wanted to give up? Make sure that students prepare a series of questions prior to interviewing their parents.

Thomas Edison Story

Thomas Edison invented the incandescent light bulb, but when he was only 7 years old, his teacher said he was too stupid to learn. As Edison pursued his invention, he tried more than 2,000 experiments before he got the electric bulb to work. A young reporter asked him how it felt to fail so many times. Edison's response? "I never failed once. I invented the light bulb. It just happened to be a 2,000-step process."

✳✳✳✳✳

My Own Success Story

_____

_____

_____

_____

_____

_____

_____

_____

_____

_____

_____

_____

_____

_____

_____

_____

_____

_____

ACTIVITY 3   Fly Away

In order to understand the value of perseverance, students need opportunities to persevere. Clearly, perseverance is important when it comes to academics, but it is also important when pursuing excellence in sports, music, or any other activities that students may want to tackle. This activity involves making paper airplanes, an exercise that most youngsters enjoy immensely.

Materials
► An instruction book on making paper airplanes
► Paper

Instructions
1. Without giving them any instructions, have your students try to build the best paper airplane they can.
2. Once the students have made their planes, give them the opportunity to fly them. Make sure to note how far the planes fly.
3. Give students a second chance, prompting them to improve the design of their planes. It is OK if students help each other and learn from each other.
4. Give students a set of directions for making paper airplanes. (These instructions are readily available in books or on the Internet.) Have students design a variety of planes.
5. After the new planes have been built, once again allow students to fly their planes.
6. Note how far the planes fly and whether they fly farther than the original planes.

Discussion
1. What did you learn after you built your first plane?
2. What did you find frustrating about this activity?
3. Did you get better at making planes? If so, how did that feel?

Enrichment
Let your class sponsor a schoolwide plane-flying contest and have them set and distribute the rules. See if local businesses will chip in prizes for the winners.

ACTIVITY 4   My Achievements

Adults and children often fail to recognize all that they have achieved in a year, a week, or even a day. This activity allows middle school students to see how much they actually have learned during a school year.

Materials
- ► My Achievements Worksheet
- ► Writing paper and pencils or pens

Instructions

1. Ask students to think back to when they first learned to ride a bike or to swim:

    What was that achievement like?

    Does it seem like a big deal now?

2. Give each student the My Achievements Worksheet.

3. Ask students to think about their achievements during the current school year and to list at least five of them in each column.

4. Ask students to put a star by the one achievement they are most proud of.

5. Allow students to share with the class at least one achievement from each category.

6. Be sure to congratulate your students on all their wonderful achievements.

7. Have the students give themselves a round of applause.

Discussion

1. What does it feel like to think about all your achievements?

2. What would you like to add to your list by the end of the school year?

3. What goals took you the longest to achieve? Why?

Enrichment Ask students to think about graduating from high school. What would they like to have accomplished by the time they graduate? What do they need to do to reach their goals? Who can help them be successful?

My Achievements Worksheet

Academic Achievements

1. _____
2. _____
3. _____
4. _____
5. _____
6. _____
7. _____
8. _____
9. _____
10. _____

Extracurricular Achievements

1. _____
2. _____
3. _____
4. _____
5. _____
6. _____
7. _____
8. _____
9. _____
10. _____

Personal Achievements

1. _____
2. _____
3. _____
4. _____
5. _____
6. _____
7. _____
8. _____
9. _____
10. _____

Raising Student Aspirations: Classroom Activities for Grades 6–8 © 2003 by Russell J. Quaglia and Kristine M. Fox. Champaign, IL: Research Press (800) 519-2707

ACTIVITY 5   Good Citizens

Middle school is a great time to promote good citizenship. It gives students the opportunity to put other people's needs ahead of theirs and to feel great about helping out. Citizenship projects should be yearlong endeavors and not one-shot deals.

Materials
- ► Community Service Worksheet
- ► Pencils or pens

Instructions
1. Give students the Community Service Worksheet and tell them they are about to undertake a yearlong community service project.
2. Together with your class, take the time to discuss your community's needs.
3. Have your students list on the worksheet the assets and needs of your community.
4. Remind the students that the project should be well thought out and planned before it is initiated. For example, students may have to write or visit several people beforehand.
5. Make sure students have devised a concrete plan and that everyone is involved in the project. The community service project can be undertaken in any class.

Discussion
1. Why do we need to give back to our community?
2. How does it feel to perform community service?
3. What other needs do you see that our community has?

Enrichment
Ask your students to write to a city council member or their state representative about a local issue that needs attention. Perhaps the food bank is in need of more funding or the school needs support for a building project.

Point out to your students that being a good citizen also means being an active member of the community.

Community Service Worksheet

Community Assets	Community Needs
1. _____	1. _____
2. _____	2. _____
3. _____	3. _____
4. _____	4. _____
5. _____	5. _____
6. _____	6. _____

Plans for Community Service Project

1. _____
_____
_____

2. _____
_____
_____

3. _____
_____
_____

4. _____
_____
_____

5. _____
_____
_____

6. _____
_____
_____

Raising Student Aspirations: Classroom Activities for Grades 6–8
© 2003 by Russell J. Quaglia and Kristine M. Fox. Champaign, IL: Research Press (800) 519-2707

ACTIVITY 6   **Get in Shape**

Some of the greatest examples of perseverance are provided by athletes. We often hear about their overcoming barriers to get stronger, run faster, and stay focused on their goals. This activity, which works especially well when the PE teacher becomes involved, challenges students to persevere at their own pace.

Materials ► None

Instructions
1. Ask your students to choose one area of physical fitness in which they would like to improve. The goal may be to run a full mile instead of only half a mile, do more sit-ups, hit the ball better, swim farther, and so forth. (It is most beneficial if the PE teacher helps students set their goals.)

2. Ask students to develop a plan, again preferably in concert with the PE instructor. Remind them that, to achieve their goals, they are going to have to expend a lot of effort.

3. Allow students time in PE class to work toward their goals. Perhaps the last 10 minutes of class can be devoted to this activity.

4. At the end of each week, be sure to ask your students about their progress.

Discussion
1. How difficult was it to reach your goal? Why?

2. Did you feel like giving up? Explain.

3. What did it feel like to be successful?

Enrichment Help your students create goals to become healthier. Some of their goals may pertain to their eating habits, exercise, and mental health. Each student should create his or her own healthy action plan. Invite guest speakers in to discuss health-related topics.

Most people love to play games. Games teach us that winning isn't everything and that it is important not to give up on the first try. Any game that requires students to think while they try again and again is a wonderful tool for teaching perseverance and effort.

Materials

► A variety of thinking games such as checkers, chess, backgammon, and Scrabble

Instructions

1. Ask students to think about their favorite childhood games:

   What did they like about these games?

   What games did they not like?

2. Let students know that they are going to play a game.

3. Ask students to keep a few questions in mind while they play their games. One thing students should think about is what it feels like to lose:

   Do they feel like giving up?

   Do they sometimes win when they think they are going to lose?

4. Tell students to have fun and play their games.

Discussion

1. What do games teach us about perseverance?

2. Why do you have to put forth effort to become good at playing a game?

3. What is fun about winning a game?

Enrichment

Ask students to develop their own games. Games should require students to think and be creative. Once the games are developed, students should share their games and take some time to play them.

ACTIVITY 8   **School Citizens**

Schools often recognize the importance of their students' good citizenship, as well as their involvement in community service projects. However, it is equally important for students to experience being good citizens at school every day, whether that entails volunteering for good causes, voting in school elections, helping classmates and neighbors, or involving themselves in local issues. This activity allows students to display their good citizenship skills for a great cause—their school.

Materials ▶ Optional: stationery and pencils or pens

Instructions 1. Inform your students that you would like the class to get involved in a school issue.

2. Ask your students to brainstorm issues at school that concern them. These issues may include discipline procedures, homework policies, extracurricular activities, or a new curriculum.

3. Have students find the appropriate people to talk with before they get involved. It may help them if they attend a school board meeting or write letters expressing their concern about a particular issue.

4. Offer students support and give them time to become good school citizens.

5. Make sure students take responsibility for their role in solving whatever problem they are concerned with. For example, if they are concerned about an unclean school, they need to think of ways they can help the situation.

6. Be prepared to advise students who want to talk with you about the obstacles they face and their fear of failure.

Discussion 1. How receptive to your ideas were the adults you encountered?

2. What was it like to get involved in your school's issues?

3. What other issues would you like to tackle?

Enrichment Ask students to keep a class citizenship journal in which they will record the citizenship projects or acts they undertake throughout the school year. Projects may be as simple as picking up trash or helping someone with homework.

Challenge Activities for Sense of Accomplishment

For Students
- ▶ Have students keep track of their accomplishments for an entire month. Ask them if they are proud of these accomplishments.
- ▶ Urge students to volunteer on a regular basis in your community. Have them take the time to learn about a variety of organizations before they begin their volunteer efforts. Remind them that they must be sure they can make a commitment.
- ▶ Have each student take the time to be a good citizen to a younger student. The older student may choose to read to the younger student, help out at recess, or just make sure to acknowledge the student.

For Teachers
- ▶ Create a way to acknowledge students who put forth effort every day, even though their grades do not improve.
- ▶ Attend school board, parent association, or town council meetings and make your voice heard. Make a point to get involved in decisions about your school.
- ▶ Tackle a problem that you find a bit intimidating. A good challenge would be any activity that requires you to persevere but also presents a strong possibility of failure on your part. Take the time to understand what it is like for students who struggle every day to be successful.

CHAPTER FOUR

FUN and EXCITEMENT

CONFIDENCE to TAKE ACTION

LEADERSHIP and RESPONSIBILITY

SPIRIT of ADVENTURE

CURIOSITY and CREATIVITY

FUN and EXCITEMENT

SENSE of ACCOMPLISHMENT

HEROES

BELONGING

Principal's Turn

If you were to ask most students if their principal or assistant principal has ever been a teacher, they probably would laugh. For the most part, students do not have the opportunity to get to know their administrators as educators; even less often do they laugh and share casual conversation with them. This detachment is a clear sign that administrators need to take an active part in promoting the condition of fun and excitement.

Materials   ▶ None

Instructions   1. Arrange ahead of time for students and the principal to swap roles. One day, have a couple of students work with the principal; another day, have the principal teach a class for a morning.

2. On the morning that the principal teaches the class, choose a lesson that will allow him or her to actively engage the students. This setup will give the students and the principal the opportunity to laugh and enjoy each other's company.

3. At least two students should be chosen to shadow the principal—one in the morning and one in the afternoon. When selecting your students, do not automatically choose the best-behaved students or the students who always seem to be chosen for special events.

4. Once this activity has been completed, make sure all your students send a thank-you note to the principal for participating in this event. Also, encourage the students who shadowed the principal to discuss their experiences with the class.

Discussion   1. What was it like having the principal teach for a morning?

2. What would you do differently if you were the teacher or the principal?

3. What other school job would you be interested in learning about? Why?

Enrichment   Give students the opportunity to plan and teach a lesson. Let them observe a variety of teachers so they can be better prepared to put together the best possible lesson plan.

A change of routine is a great way to inject fun and excitement into the school day. Most students excitedly anticipate the opportunity to dress up, look different, and just have fun during the school day.

Materials

▶ Optional: decorating materials

▶ Optional: a CD player and CDs of music from another country

Instructions

1. Once a month, hold a "country day" in the cafeteria. For example, one day might be Mexican day. On that day, Mexican cuisine should be served, Mexican music should be played, and the walls should be decorated with Mexican themes. Students may even want to decorate the tables.

2. Encourage duty teachers and cafeteria workers to dress the part.

3. If there is a break after lunch, introduce games from the country you are celebrating.

4. Post words in the country's language on the walls of the classroom.

5. Be sure to eat lunch with the students in the cafeteria on country days.

Discussion

1. What makes a change of routine fun and exciting?

2. How can we make our class routines more fun and exciting?

3. What one school routine would you change?

Enrichment

In individual classes, undertake projects that relate to the theme of the country being celebrated. The projects may include learning about dances and other customs unique to that country. Decorate the school's entranceway and engage in a daylong, schoolwide celebration of the country you have chosen.

ACTIVITY 3   **Fun with Words**

It is often challenging to help students become more creative and excited about learning. After all, when they are very young, students are given guidelines that help them learn the way things should be done. Any activity that encourages students to broaden their thinking will help promote the condition of fun and excitement. This activity is especially helpful to students prior to a writing assignment.

Materials   ▶ None

Instructions   1. You probably have noticed a few words that your students tend to overuse in their writing. For example, students may use the verb *walked* too often when they describe motion. Write this word on the chalkboard, along with other words you deem forbidden—at least for the time being—and inform students that their writing may not include these words.

2. To get the creative juices flowing, ask students to form a line on one side of the room and tell them that they are going to take part in a creativity contest. The challenge will be for students to fill in the blank with an alternative verb:

   Using their own name, they must say, for example, "Sam _____ across the room."

   Although the verb they use to fill in the blank must indicate movement across the room, that verb may not be *walked*. In this example, Sam might have strolled, strutted, meandered, or run across the room.

3. As you instruct your students, tell them they not only have to fill in the blank with a verb other than *walked,* but must also perform the motion they describe. Other aspects of the activity:

   Instruct those students who cannot think of a substitute for *walked* to sit down.

   As each student in line takes his or her turn choosing a word, write that word on the chalkboard.

   Once the students have chosen a word and performed the motion indicated by that word, encourage them to go to the end of the line and wait their next turn to call out a word.

   Make the winner the last student who comes up with a creative alternative to *walked.*

4. At the end of the activity, have the students look at the words you have written on the chalkboard so they can see the many alternatives to *walked.*

Discussion
1. Why is it so difficult to break speaking and writing routines?
2. How else can we be more creative in our writing?
3. What are some fun topics you would like to write about?

Enrichment
During a writing assignment, challenge your students not to use the same verb twice.

ACTIVITY 4   Balloons

It is fairly common to hear students utter the words "I'm bored." By doing something different or unusual, you can help break the cycle of boredom. This activity provides you with a fun way to assign homework or even in-class tasks. It requires little preparation and can be done anytime, although it works best on special occasions or at the end of the school week.

Materials
- ▶ Balloons
- ▶ Slips of paper

Instructions
1. On slips of paper, write several alternative homework assignments. For example, you may choose to instruct students to complete only the even-numbered math problems in their textbook, or perhaps only problems 1–10. You may even want to write, "No homework," on a slip.

2. Blow up as many balloons as assignments you have written, but before blowing up the balloons, insert one assignment slip in each.

3. When it is time to assign homework, ask one student to select a balloon and pop it to retrieve the homework assignment written on the slip of paper. Whichever assignment slip floats out of the popped balloon should be the assignment for the entire class.

Discussion
1. What activities do you find boring?
2. How can we make boring activities more fun and exciting?
3. How can we make learning more fun?

Enrichment
Another fun activity is to allow students to help create unit tests or quizzes. Assign students the task of writing three or four questions for an upcoming quiz. Prior to administering the quiz, collect all the students' questions and use them to make up the quiz.

ACTIVITY 5   **Music Video**

Although musical tastes change from generation to generation, almost all students find the music of the day to be fun and exciting. Students are usually able to relate to the messages relayed through musical lyrics while, at the same time, enjoying the mental relaxation that music provides.

Materials
► Writing paper and pencils or pens
► Videotaping equipment

Instructions
1. Inform the class that they have been contacted by a popular recording star who wants them to complete the following assignment: Create music videos that relate to your subject matter.

2. The subject you are studying will, of course, dictate the theme of the videos. For example, if the students are studying history, then the videos must relate to history.

3. Divide students into groups of four and instruct them to create the lyrics, the dance moves, and the music for a video. Although students may use current music, they must think up their own lyrics. The lyrics should be factual.

4. Obtain the necessary video equipment and help your students tape their videos and present them as music videos that youngsters are used to watching on TV. You may want to act as the host and play up the introductions. The idea is to have fun.

Discussion
1. Why do so many students like music videos?
2. If you could be a famous singer, who would you like to be and why?
3. What was the most difficult part of making the video?

Enrichment
Invite a guest speaker to your classroom to discuss video and TV production.

Let your students experiment with different video productions.

Take your class on a tour of a TV studio.

ACTIVITY 6   Fun with Modeling Clay

By the time they reach middle school, most students have put away their modeling clay, toys, and kids' games. Still, having the opportunity to take part in younger children's activities is fun for everyone. Allowing students just to be kids again is a great way to help them relax and have fun.

Materials
► Modeling clay, crayons, finger-painting supplies, and kids' toys and games

Instructions
1. Fill a box full of fun items. The box should contain items that students remember playing with when they were younger.
2. Let students know that, whenever they finish taking a major exam, they will be given 5 minutes to play with something from the fun box.
3. Encourage the students to be creative and to enjoy themselves.
4. Invite students to add toys and games to the fun box.

Discussion
1. What activity do you remember enjoying the most when you were in kindergarten?
2. What do you miss the most about being in elementary school?
3. How can we have more fun in middle school?

Enrichment
Allow students to build and create more often.

Include artistic assignments in math and writing classes.

ACTIVITY 7   **Go Fly a Kite**

A great way to promote the condition of fun and excitement is to allow students time to explore the arts. Introducing arts and hands-on lessons in math and other traditional paper-and-pencil classes will engage and excite students.

Materials
- ▶ Books about kite building
- ▶ Materials for building a kite
- ▶ Art supplies

Instructions

1. Challenge your students to build a kite. In order for the kites to fly, students will have to explore what dimensions work best, what materials should be used, and other relevant information.

2. Give students enough time to plan their kite building and decorating.

3. Provide students with the necessary supplies to build and decorate their kites.

4. Once the kites are completed, take the students outside and give them ample time to fly their kites. You may even want to invite a younger class of students to enjoy an hour of kite flying with the older students.

Discussion

1. What did you learn about kite flying?

2. How could you make your kite stay aloft longer next time?

3. What was fun about this activity?

Enrichment

Take some time to learn about flying. For example, how do planes and kites and birds fly?

Come up with questions about flying that your students will have to answer.

ACTIVITY 8   Story Creation

Knowing how to help students have fun while writing and learning is an invaluable tool. This activity enables students to develop their creativity while they also learn to enjoy writing.

Materials   ▶ Writing paper and pencils or pens

Instructions   1. Give each student a piece of paper and a pencil.

2. Inform your students that they are going to create a story and that you will be giving them words that they are to include in the story.

3. Give the students a few minutes to write a two-sentence opener to their story. Encourage students to be creative.

4. Give the students a noun, a verb, or whatever word you decide on and have them use this word in their next sentence. Encourage the students to create a story that makes sense.

5. Allow the students to write a few more sentences on their own and then introduce a new word. After you have introduced three or four words, call on a student to introduce another word. Continue this exercise until six or seven words have been introduced.

6. Allow time for students to share their stories in small groups.

Discussion   1. What makes writing assignments boring?

2. How can you improve your own writing?

3. What makes a story exciting and engaging?

Enrichment   Compose several stories about a paragraph or two in length. Omit words throughout the stories, substituting blanks for the omitted words. Ask students to fill in the blanks on copies of the stories with creative, fun words.

Challenge Activities for Fun and Excitement

For Students

► Encourage students to stay after school and just play. They may choose to shoot hoops with friends or play kick ball, soccer, or some other game.

► Invite students to take pictures of their friends and create a collage. Have them photocopy the collage and give each of their friends a copy.

► Allow students to listen to music at the end of the week while doing an assignment. Introduce students to a variety of music.

For Teachers

► Take the time to laugh with your colleagues. Introduce lunchtime themes, music, and fun.

► Take charge of your next staff meeting and make it fun. Make sure you get people up and moving. Do not permit colleagues to sit together in the same groups.

► Dress up in the style of the era when you are studying a specific period in history or a literary figure of the time.

CHAPTER FIVE

CURIOSITY and CREATIVITY

CONFIDENCE to TAKE ACTION

LEADERSHIP and RESPONSIBILITY

SPIRIT of ADVENTURE

CURIOSITY and CREATIVITY

FUN and EXCITEMENT

SENSE of ACCOMPLISHMENT

HEROES

BELONGING

ACTIVITY 1   Mystery Picture

The condition of curiosity and creativity encourages us to look at the world through a different lens. Just because something has always been done one way does not mean it cannot be done another way. Promoting curiosity and creativity will allow your students to see their world in wonderful new ways.

Materials
▶ A variety of magazines

Instructions
1. Search through magazines such as *National Geographic* that feature vivid pictures.

2. Choose a variety of pictures that, initially, are not identifiable. For example, one picture may be a close-up of a blade of grass.

3. Tell students that you are going to hold a contest once a week that will involve writing about a picture. Tell them, however, that the student who comes up with the correct answer will not be declared the winner. The winner, instead, will be the student who comes up with the most creative, unique identification. (This activity will be a real challenge for some students because they have been conditioned to answer questions correctly, rather than creatively.)

4. Allow students the opportunity to share their creative and inspirational ideas with the class.

Discussion
1. Why is it difficult not to be concerned about the one and only answer?

2. Can you think of a question that has more than one right answer?

3. What does it mean to stretch your imagination?

Enrichment
Allow your students to take their own mystery pictures with a camera and post them in the classroom.

On a bulletin board, post your students' mystery pictures. Also post guesses by students who are trying to identify the subject of the picture.

If you do not have access to cameras, have students draw their mystery pictures instead.

ACTIVITY 2   What's in a Name?

Names and nicknames have much meaning and significance. Some people are named after relatives, whereas others are named by parents who fell in love with the name when they first heard it. Exploring names and their origins will stir the curiosity of even the most indifferent students. This activity explores the history and the meaning of the names of your students.

Materials
- ► Baby-name books
- ► Slips of paper and pencils or pens

Instructions

1. Ask students if they know what their names mean. If they do not know, ask them to guess the meaning, write it on a slip of paper, and give it to you.

2. Place a variety of baby-name books around the room so students can find out the meaning of their names.

3. Once again, ask students to write down the meaning of their names, but insist that they don't let their classmates see the meaning. Have students write the meaning on a slip of paper and give it to you.

4. Ask the class to guess which meanings go with which students: Do the meanings make sense for those classmates?

Discussion

1. Why did your parents choose your name?

2. What is your favorite name for a boy and for a girl?

3. What surprised you about the meaning of your name?

Enrichment

Ask your students to write their names vertically on a piece of paper. Next, have them think about themselves and their personalities. Then have them think about a word that describes themselves and that begins with each letter of their name. For example, Sam might consider himself *s*illy, *a*thletic, and *m*usical. Give students the opportunity to share their descriptions with the class.

ACTIVITY 3   What's in the Bag?

It is often difficult for middle school students to engage in original thought. They are used to seeing the world one way, and, in their opinion, that is the way things should be. This activity promotes creativity and encourages students to think a bit differently by having them offer original thoughts about the contents of half a dozen bags.

Materials
▶ Three Questions Worksheet
▶ 6 lunch bags
▶ Small, random items to put in the bags

Instructions
1. Put a random selection of items (e.g., marbles, tissue, paper clips, candy) in each of the six lunch bags and number them from 1 to 6.

2. Give students the Three Questions Worksheet and tell them they are to answer the same three questions for each bag. Be sure to inform them that you are not looking for the right answer but rather a creative and interesting answer. (Although you may allow the students to shake the bags or lift them to check their weight, you may not permit them to look inside the bags or feel their contents.)

3. Do not give the students any hints or suggestions; let their imaginations run wild.

4. Once the students have finished the assignment, collect the Three Questions Worksheets and read the students' answers aloud. After you read each answer for each bag, disclose to the class the actual contents of the bag. (It is always fun if the No. 6 bag contains candy so you can share some sweets with the class at the end of the activity.)

Discussion
1. Why was it difficult not to write down the "right" answers?
2. Why did the answers vary so widely?
3. Is it fun or difficult to be creative? Why or why not?

Enrichment
Try the same activity again, but this time allow students to see the objects in the bags and ponder, for example, What else could a pencil be? What could it be used for?

Three Questions Worksheet

Question	Bag 1	Bag 2	Bag 3	Bag 4	Bag 5	Bag 6
What is in the bag?						
How did it get in there?						
What can the item be used for?						

Raising Student Aspirations: Classroom Activities for Grades 6–8 © 2003 by Russell J. Quaglia and Kristine M. Fox. Champaign, IL: Research Press (800) 519-2707

ACTIVITY 4   **Cultural Exploration**

One of the most exciting ways to explore curiosity and creativity is to learn about different cultures. Students are always amazed and in awe of the different foods, dress, dances, and traditions of people from around the world. This activity can be as extensive as you desire.

Materials   ▶ A globe or a map of the world

Instructions   1. Together with your students, brainstorm the various ways that cultures differ. For example, what is different about the food, language, art, religion, climate, transportation, and so on?

2. Let students look at a globe or a map of the world. Ask them to name aloud countries they have never heard of or know little about. Write these on the chalkboard and then choose one country to explore in depth.

3. Have students explore the unique cultural characteristics of the country you have chosen and ask them to put together a profile of the country.

Discussion   1. What surprised you the most about the country?

2. How are the people like us? How are they different?

3. Would you like to live there? Why or why not?

Enrichment   Divide students into small groups and give them the opportunity to create their own country. Instruct them to create 10 characteristics of their country, such as climate, locale, industry, foods, and the like. Have the students consolidate this information into a presentation. Depending on the time available, encourage the students to design a flag for their country and also to write a national anthem.

ACTIVITY 5　　　Unusual Stories

Given the opportunity and enough encouragement, middle school students can come up with wonderfully creative and exciting ideas. This writing activity encourages students to be creative and curious about everyday items.

Materials ► Writing paper and pencils or pens

Instructions

1. Prior to engaging your students in this activity, think of one everyday item—a plate, a shirt, a pen, a desk—for each person in the class.

2. Together with your class, brainstorm the following: a list of action words (at least one word per student) and a variety of settings (at least one setting per student).

3. Inform the students that their assignment is to write a short story, but with a few qualifications:

   Each student should be given an everyday item, an action word, and a setting, all of which must appear in his or her story.

   The item must be the central character, but this item (or central character) may not represent the name of a person. For example, John's nickname cannot be *pencil*.

   Encourage the students to write funny, sad, or mystery stories.

4. Because of the need for revision and editing, this activity may take several class periods to complete. Or you may decide to make it a quick exercise in which students present their stories orally.

5. Have students share their stories and try to guess the identities of the main characters.

Discussion

1. What was challenging about this activity?
2. What do you like or dislike about writing? Why?
3. What topic do you find interesting to write about?

Enrichment

This same type of activity can be done through artwork. Students should either choose or be given an everyday item. They must then create a masterpiece by drawing or painting just that single item. (To inspire your students, you may want to show them Andy Warhol's famous paintings that consist merely of Campbell Soup cans.) Some students may want to create 3-D images.

ACTIVITY 6   Historical Characters

Exploring history can be exciting and intriguing for some students, whereas for others, it may seem mundane and routine. This activity lends a new twist to studying a specific period in history and can be incorporated into whatever unit you are currently studying in history or social studies. It allows students to learn about a different era from a different point of view.

Materials   ▶ History or social studies textbooks

Instructions
1. Have students begin by thinking of famous people who are either dead or alive. These people may include U.S. presidents, philanthropists, sports figures, or anyone else the students deem important or famous.

2. Each student should select one famous person and then write about what life would be like for this person if he or she were alive during the time period you are studying. For example, what would life have been like for Martin Luther King, Jr., if he had been alive during the Civil War?

   This activity will require research and in-depth exploration. After all, many questions will take on new meaning: What would have been different about King's daily life if he had lived in the North rather than the South? What foods would he have eaten? What clothes would he have worn? What would his livelihood have been? What kind of friends would he have had?

3. This project should provide you with a new and unique way to assess students' true understanding of a particular time period and what life was like back then.

Discussion
1. What would be the biggest obstacle facing your character?
2. What would your biggest obstacle have been if you had lived in that time period?
3. What would you like to see changed sometime in the future?

Enrichment   Have students place their characters in the future: What would life be like for them? How would life be better or worse? What issues would they face in the future?

Remember to encourage creativity.

Music seems to be the one common language of teenagers. Music never seems to get boring, old, or loud enough. Students are curious about lyrics and enjoy creating their own rhythms, songs, and dances.

Materials
▶ A CD player

▶ CDs of purely instrumental music

▶ Optional: videotaping equipment

Instructions
1. Inform your students that you have been contacted by a major record label to help create lyrics to music and you would like the class to help you.

2. Let your students listen to half a dozen musical selections. Some music may sound funny without visuals or words, such as the theme to a popular TV show; others, such as the national anthem, may set a more somber tone. Be sure to play a few songs whose lyrics the students are unfamiliar with.

3. When you play songs that the students are familiar with, ask the students to try not to think of the actual lyrics.

4. Divide the class into small groups and assign each group a musical selection. Tell them their task is to create lyrics to the music. (The students whose task it is to write words to a very popular or familiar selection actually have a tougher task; they need to forget about the lyrics that are running through their heads.)

5. Give the students enough time to create, practice, and perform. If you have the equipment, you may want to videotape the creations and show them to the class. This addition to the activity will allow all the students to enjoy these musical masterpieces.

Discussion
1. How difficult was it to be creative with this activity?

2. Do you think musicians develop lyrics first or music first? Why?

3. If you could meet one famous musician, who would it be and why?

Enrichment
Challenge your students to write their own musical scores. Students who are not familiar with musical notes should be introduced to the basic scale and a few easy songs.

ACTIVITY 8   Questions and Answers

The condition of curiosity and creativity invites students to ask questions, discover answers, and thoroughly enjoy learning. This activity encourages students to formulate good questions and to practice asking them so they can become better engaged in the learning process.

Materials   ► None

Instructions
1. Inform students that the class is going to play a question-and-answer game and that you are going to get the ball rolling by thinking of a person, place, or thing.
2. Tell students that their task is to ask as few yes-or-no questions as possible en route to figuring out who or what you have in mind.
3. As the class becomes proficient at this activity, have them ask yes-or-no questions that pertain to the subject matter they are studying. For example, if you are teaching social studies, think of a person, place, or thing you have been discussing. As students ask questions, they will be reviewing the material and having fun at the same time.
4. As you revisit this activity during the course of the year, give each student the opportunity to think of a person, place, or thing. Join your students in asking questions.

Discussion
1. What types of questions helped the class find the answers the quickest?
2. Why is it important to ask good questions?
3. How else, besides asking questions, can we find answers to the questions we are curious about?

Enrichment   Prior to beginning a unit of study, ask students to think about things they would like to know about the subject matter. If you are studying volcanoes, for example, have each student think of five questions about volcanoes that he or she would like to find the answers to before the unit is over. This activity is a great way to involve students in lesson development.

Challenge Activities for Curiosity and Creativity

For Students

▶ Have students explore a subject they have never studied in school before, such as psychology or astrology.

▶ Challenge students to complete a research paper or project by interviewing people who are knowledgeable about the subject matter.

▶ Challenge students to explore the arts. Encourage them to take classes in art, dance, or music.

For Teachers

▶ Throw out old lesson plans. Develop new lesson plans that use current information.

▶ Offer students a variety of options for completing an assignment. Take the time to learn about multiple intelligences before you develop your assignments.

▶ Encourage your students to explore their artistic side—even in math or science.

CHAPTER SIX

SPIRIT of ADVENTURE

CONFIDENCE to TAKE ACTION

LEADERSHIP and RESPONSIBILITY

SPIRIT of ADVENTURE

CURIOSITY and CREATIVITY

FUN and EXCITEMENT

SENSE of ACCOMPLISHMENT

HEROES

BELONGING

ACTIVITY 1   Goal Setting

Anyone who has spent time talking to middle school students knows that they are often not very organized. Goal-setting skills can help these students organize their schoolwork and time. As this activity shows, the condition of spirit of adventure promotes healthy goal-setting skills.

Materials
- ▶ Goal-Setting Worksheet
- ▶ Pencils or pens

Instructions

1. Discuss goal setting with your students and explain that they should be allowed to set their own goals. Let the class know that each student is going to set one academic goal.

2. Explain to the class the following goal-setting guidelines: Goals must be achievable, measurable, meaningful, and specific.

3. Give your students the Goal-Setting Worksheet and allow them enough time to think about their goal and record it on the worksheet. Each day, they are to write down the steps they have taken toward reaching their goal.

4. Each week, distribute the Goal-Setting Worksheet to your students, have them evaluate their progress toward their goal, and then collect all the worksheets.

5. Meet individually with your students throughout the week to discuss their progress.

6. Make sure to celebrate when each student achieves his or her goal.

Discussion

1. What is difficult about goal setting?
2. What does it feel like to achieve your goal?
3. What long-term goals do you have?

Enrichment

Develop short-, medium-, and long-term goals with your students.

Pair up students and have partner help partner progress and eventually reach his or her goal.

Goal-Setting Worksheet

Student: _____

Goal: _____

Week of: _____

Monday	Tuesday	Wednesday	Thursday	Friday

Raising Student Aspirations: Classroom Activities for Grades 6–8 © 2003 by Russell J. Quaglia and Kristine M. Fox. Champaign, IL: Research Press (800) 519-2707

ACTIVITY 2   Ideal Job

As students begin to think about their future, it is important for them to understand the skills they will need once they finish school and enter the workplace. The condition of spirit of adventure challenges students to think about their future and the skills they need to reach their goals. This activity encourages students to begin thinking about their careers. Therefore, it is recommended that students scour employment brochures or classified ads in the newspaper before they begin this activity.

Materials
- ▶ Ideal Job Worksheet
- ▶ Optional: employment brochures
- ▶ Optional: classified ads from various newspapers

Instructions
1. Give students the Ideal Job Worksheet.
2. Have them think of three ideal jobs and list each one separately:

   In the first column, they should list the job. In the second column, they should list five skills they consider necessary to do the job properly. In the third column, they should list the ways they can acquire those five skills.

3. Once they have completed the worksheet, make sure you take the time to discuss job choices and skills with your students.

Discussion
1. What do you feel will be your greatest career challenge?
2. What do you think would be an exciting and rewarding career?
3. How much schooling is required for your chosen career?

Enrichment
Arrange to have some of your students job shadow. Solicit parents' and community members' help in pairing students with their job interests. Make sure students are prepared with questions and ready to learn when they go visit and observe adults in the workplace.

Ideal Job Worksheet

Job	Five Necessary Skills	How to Acquire Skills
1.	1. 2. 3. 4. 5.	
2.	1. 2. 3. 4. 5.	
3.	1. 2. 3. 4. 5.	

ACTIVITY 3   **Healthy Risk Taking**

There are many ways to take risks every day. Students often find themselves in situations that require them to choose between taking good risks or bad risks. For example, students may have to choose whether or not to finish their homework, whether to fight back when confronted by someone or merely walk away, or whether to pay attention in class or goof off. This activity introduces students to a number of ways they can take healthy risks at school every day.

Materials
- ► Risk-Taking Worksheet
- ► Pencils or pens

Instructions
1. Together with your students, brainstorm ways to take healthy risks at school. Staying out of trouble and studying during lunchtime are two examples of healthy risks. Push your students to think about all the risks they take every day.

2. Give students the Risk-Taking Worksheet and ask them to keep track of all the healthy risks they take in one week at school. Have them also note all the opportunities they have to take unhealthy risks.

3. At the end of the week, let students share the risks they took.

Discussion
1. Did you have more opportunities at school to take healthy risks or unhealthy risks? Explain.

2. Why is it important to push yourself to take healthy risks?

3. What is the most challenging risk you have ever taken?

Enrichment
Assign each student a healthy risk to take. For example, you might assign students who never speak up in class to take the risk of raising their hand twice a day. Or you might assign students who are always talking to take the risk of listening and being quiet. Reward those students who meet the challenge of taking healthy risks.

Risk-Taking Worksheet

Healthy Risks Taken	Opportunities to Take Unhealthy Risks
1.	1.
2.	2.
3.	3.
4.	4.
5.	5.
6.	6.
7.	7.
8.	8.
9.	9.
10.	10.

Raising Student Aspirations: Classroom Activities for Grades 6–8
© 2003 by Russell J. Quaglia and Kristine M. Fox. Champaign, IL: Research Press (800) 519-2707

ACTIVITY 4   Student Report Cards

Most report cards consist solely of teachers' evaluations of students and do not allow the space or opportunity for students to self-evaluate and set goals for the next term. This activity emphasizes the importance of allowing students to evaluate their personal growth so they can take ownership of and responsibility for their schoolwork.

Materials
- A self-evaluation form of your choosing
- Pencils or pens

Instructions
1. Ask students to think about their schoolwork and social interactions at school and tell them that part of their report card is going to be created by them.
2. Give students a self-evaluation form at the end of the quarter and have them fill it out. Let them know that their self-evaluation will be sent to their parents as part of their report card and that it should be considered an important evaluation component.
3. Meet with students to discuss this self-evaluation component. If there is a marked discrepancy between a student's self-evaluation and your evaluation, you may need to discuss the situation further.
4. Before the start of the next quarter, have students review their goals from their most recent self-evaluation and update them as necessary.

Discussion
1. What was it like evaluating yourself?
2. Why is it important for you to evaluate your work?
3. How did your evaluation differ from the teacher's?

Enrichment
Invite students to be an active part of student-parent conferences. Students should present their work, their goals, and their ideas for improvement. The more responsibility students have, the more ownership they will take of their grades and work.

ACTIVITY 5   Magic Tricks

Although many students consider giving a class presentation a wonderful experience, other students consider it a big risk. This activity helps students develop their presentation skills and perhaps increase their self-confidence.

Materials
- ▶ Books about magic tricks
- ▶ A banner, construction paper and markers, and other decorating materials
- ▶ Optional: a CD player and CDs
- ▶ Optional: a VCR and a videotape of magicians performing tricks

Instructions
1. Let your students know that they are going to have the opportunity to perform a magic trick for the class and then teach everyone the secret to their trick.
2. Make sure you give students enough time to find a trick they like, practice it, and then rehearse it in front of a small group. Also allow time for students to gather materials for their magic trick.
3. Create a banner introducing the class's magic show and set the stage with music and other signs. You may even want to show a short video featuring famous magicians prior to beginning.
4. Allow each student time to shine on stage.

Discussion
1. What do you find difficult about speaking in front of the class?
2. Why is it easy for some people to speak in public?
3. How does practice help prepare you for a group presentation?

Enrichment
Ask students to develop theories of how some of the most famous magic tricks in the world are done. For example, how do magicians levitate people or make items appear or disappear? Tell students that you are looking for creative and interesting answers—not necessarily the correct answers.

Teach the Class

Teachers often forget that their classes include students who are experts on certain topics—that everyone has something to teach. Using students as resources is a great way to promote learning and also to build students' risk-taking confidence.

Materials   ▶ Writing paper and pencils or pens

Instructions
1. Begin this activity by asking students to think about all their skills, talents, interests, and hobbies, which may range from cooking to sports to geography.

2. On the chalkboard, list 10 categories of activities that require certain skills.

3. Have your students list on a piece of paper the skills they possess that are associated with any or all of the categories you have posted.

4. After you have collected the students' inventories, list under each category heading on the board the names of students and the skills they possess. Doing so will help you later, when you need to call on your students for their expertise.

5. Let the students know that they may be asked to teach the class whenever their skills are needed in a particular area.

6. Find opportunities throughout the year to use all your student experts.

Discussion
1. What is something new you learned about a classmate's skills?

2. What new skill would you most like to learn?

3. How can your skills be helpful to others?

Enrichment   Help students create a log of their current skills and those skills they wish to obtain in the future. Once a month let students update their log and share what they have learned both in and out of school. This log can then be shared with the next year's teacher prior to the beginning of the school year.

ACTIVITY 7   Learn Something New

Learning something new and potentially difficult can be risky for students of any age, many of whom may fear failure. Students need to be encouraged to challenge and push themselves to learn whenever possible. The spirit of adventure will flourish if students are willing to take risks.

Materials
- Books, magazines, newspapers, or other sources of information
- Writing paper and pencils or pens

Instructions
1. Ask students to think of a variety of questions they would like to know the answers to. For the purpose of this activity, the questions should be concrete and not too philosophical or open-ended.
2. On the chalkboard, list each student's questions and write the name of the questioner next to each question.
3. Pair up students and have them find the answers to one or two of the questions. Make sure that no two groups are exploring the same question, and give students sufficient time to research their answers.
4. For added fun, have students ask questions of adults inside and outside the school and record their answers.
5. Once students have come up with their answers, have them share them with the class.

Discussion
1. What was the most interesting thing you learned about your question?
2. Was it difficult to find answers? Why or why not?
3. Would you think about finding answers to other intriguing questions in the future? Why or why not?

Enrichment
Once a week, create a teacher challenge question. Give students a week to find the answer by themselves and turn it in to you. Award points or stars to students for each correct answer. At the end of the month, tally points and celebrate the students' quest for knowledge.

ACTIVITY 8   Understanding Your Challenges

It is important for students of all ages to set and reach goals. One of the biggest obstacles to creating meaningful goals is students' inability to understand how to achieve their goals. An important step in learning how to reach their goals is for students to understand what it is that they find challenging and to learn how to overcome that challenge. This activity encourages students to reflect on a number of challenges they may face at school every day.

Materials
- ► Understanding Your Challenges Worksheet
- ► Pencils or pens

Instructions
1. Give students the Understanding Your Challenges Worksheet and instruct them to read each challenge and place a check mark in the column that best describes their feelings about the challenge. Tell them that, at the bottom of the worksheet, they are to answer the three questions.
2. Offer to help your students meet their challenges and achieve their goals.

Discussion
1. Why are some tasks easy for some students yet difficult for others?
2. What challenges did you face when you were younger that you no longer have to confront?
3. How can we all help each other confront our challenges?

Enrichment
At the end of each day, have your students think about the challenges they faced and how they handled those challenges. Ask them to keep a journal of their challenges for an entire week. By encouraging students to think about the challenges they face every day, you will help them to become better able to deal with their challenges.

Understanding Your Challenges Worksheet

Challenge	Easy	OK	Difficult
1. Making new friends			
2. Speaking in front of groups			
3. Working on group projects			
4. Disagreeing with others			
5. Sharing my writing			
6. Raising my hand in class			
7. Listening to others' ideas			
8. Being picked last for a team			
9. Sitting at lunch without my friends			
10. Seeking help after school			
11. Memorizing facts			
12. Completing long projects			

What do you consider your most challenging task?

_____

_____

Why is this task challenging?

_____

_____

What goal can you set to make this task easier for you to accomplish?

_____

_____

Raising Student Aspirations: Classroom Activities for Grades 6–8
© 2003 by Russell J. Quaglia and Kristine M. Fox. Champaign, IL: Research Press (800) 519-2707

Challenge Activities for Spirit of Adventure

For Students

► Challenge students to take the difficult course, do extra problems, read a difficult book. Students are almost always surprised at how easy the "difficult" challenges really are.

► Have students create two or three personal goals they would like to achieve sometime during the school year, such as making new friends, trying out for a sports team, or completing homework on time.

► Encourage students to be vocal about a school issue that concerns them, such as the school's intention to cut classroom supplies, fire a coach, or build an addition to the school. Urge them to take risks and get involved so that adults know that their voice matters.

For Teachers

► Vow to make your teaching goals meaningful this year. Choose one or two goals, measure your progress, create benchmarks, and let this be a year of meaningful goal setting.

► Teach something new this year. No matter what your subject is, there is always something new and exciting to learn and teach. Let your students know the risk you are taking and ask them for feedback on the new subject matter.

► Invite a colleague or two into your class to evaluate your teaching and interactions with students. Constructive criticism is a wonderful learning tool and also exemplifies spirit of adventure.

CHAPTER SEVEN

LEADERSHIP and RESPONSIBILITY

CONFIDENCE to TAKE ACTION

LEADERSHIP and RESPONSIBILITY

SPIRIT of ADVENTURE

CURIOSITY and CREATIVITY

FUN and EXCITEMENT

SENSE of ACCOMPLISHMENT

HEROES

BELONGING

Many leaders are good negotiators because they understand that compromise is important and involves a lot of give-and-take. This fun activity encourages students to negotiate the sale of a product.

Materials   ▶ Everyday Item Cards

Instructions   1. Provide enough Everyday Item Cards for the entire class and stack them facedown in a pile.

2. Have students select a card and then begin to think of ways to market the item, or product, that's written on it.

3. Encourage students to find out what their classmates are selling so that they can better promote their own product.

4. Have students create persuasive sales pitches and displays. Encourage students to have fun and be creative and original—the construction of a new school playground is dependent on the sale of their product.

Discussion   1. Which products would you purchase? Why?

2. What makes for a good sales pitch?

3. How does this activity relate to leadership?

Enrichment   Ask students to create a sales pitch for something they want at school. The students should try to convince administrators or a parents' group to purchase it for the school.

Everyday Item Cards

10 pencils	4 paper cups	6 straws
2 rulers	1 yardstick	3 chairs
1 dozen eggs	1 computer keyboard	6 oranges
6 apples	2 ballpoint pens	1 fountain pen
10 envelopes	4 folders	2 candy bars
1 data disk	8 refrigerator magnets	6 rolls of paper towels
3 spoons	3 forks	3 napkins
15 erasers	7 bananas	8 notebooks

Raising Student Aspirations: Classroom Activities for Grades 6–8
© 2003 by Russell J. Quaglia and Kristine M. Fox. Champaign, IL: Research Press (800) 519-2707

ACTIVITY 2   Building Debating Skills

The ability to communicate is a valuable skill for leaders because, in order to be effective leaders, they must be able to make themselves understood through both the spoken word and the written word. Although students often have strong opinions and are very passionate about them, they tend to lack the skills to express their views clearly and thoughtfully. This activity engages students in mock debates that should hone their communication skills.

Materials   ▶ Writing paper and pencils or pens

Instructions   1. Before beginning the activity, think of a number of controversial school issues, such as the following: Should all students be required to adhere to a dress code? Should school be in session year round? Should the school day be lengthened? Should the football program be eliminated because it is too expensive to maintain?

2. Inform your students that they have been elected to represent the school and must debate a variety of school issues convincingly by thinking clearly and being well organized.

3. Divide the class into an even number of small groups.

4. Randomly assign each group one side of a debatable issue. (Note that students will find this activity more challenging if they are not allowed to choose which side of an issue they wish to debate.)

5. Give each group 20 minutes to come up with an argument that supports their side of the issue.

6. Give each group 5 minutes to present their side of the story.

Discussion   1. What constitutes a good debate?

2. What is difficult about debating?

3. What could you do better the next time you debate an issue?

Enrichment   Introduce your class to formal debating rules. Ask students to follow these guidelines and engage in debates on a monthly basis.

Allow your students the opportunity to watch a debate or observe the actions of a dynamic decision-making group.

ACTIVITY 3   The Needs of Others

One characteristic of good leaders is that they understand the needs of others. Good leaders also must know why they were chosen to be leaders. Student leaders often are chosen because they are nice or because people respect them. Some leaders are chosen because they are viewed as tough or strong; however, these leaders usually have little understanding of the responsibilities that go with being a leader.

Materials
▶ Writing paper and pencils or pens

Instructions

1. Lead a class discussion about the needs that all humans have—no matter where they live, where they work, or how much money they earn.

2. Let students know that, as a leader, it is important to understand the needs of the people who follow or respect you.

3. Divide students into small groups and have them brainstorm the needs of various groups, keeping in mind the following:

   Each group of students must represent a certain segment of society (e.g., senior citizens, parents, kindergartners, business-people).

   Each group should try to be as creative as possible in deciding on their identity.

4. Inform the class that your community is considering raising taxes to fund a new school building. Have each group make a case for or against the tax hike and present it to the rest of the class. (You may want to choose an issue that is causing controversy in your community.)

Discussion

1. Which group of people do you think is listened to the least?

2. What does it feel like not to have your opinions and ideas heard?

3. How can students become more active in their school and community?

Enrichment

Ask students to interview people from various groups. What are their issues and concerns? How does one group's issues differ from another's? How do these differences among groups make decision making difficult? Why is it beneficial to have many different groups comprise a community?

ACTIVITY 4　　　**The New Student Council**

By the time students reach middle school, student leaders have emerged from the group. The popular and more vocal students are usually elected to the student council. It is a situation that leaves many students with no opportunities to be part of a decision-making group. This activity allows all students to be part of a leadership group. In order to do this activity, teachers from all grade levels will have to be involved. Together as a group, you will decide to try something different with the student council. The goal is to include all students in the council who want to be school leaders.

Materials
- ► Leadership Contract
- ► Pencils or pens

Instructions
1. Inform students that the student council needs more members. However, before they can be on the student council, they must sign a leadership contract. The contract calls for students to be school role models, listen to others' ideas and opinions, be accepting of all students, and attend meetings. (Depending on your school's needs, these contractual requirements may have to be modified.)

2. After students sign the contract, let them know that they will be held accountable. Tell them that students who fail to live up to the conditions of the contract will be asked to leave the student council.

3. Together with your students, brainstorm as many committees as possible that would benefit the school, such as a social committee, a fund-raising committee, a pep rally committee, and a teacher-student curriculum committee. There must be enough committees so that each student has the opportunity to be part of a committee and also play a leadership role. (Have students indicate their first and second choices of committees they would like to join.)

4. Divide students into committees. Each committee should develop a specific role for each student: president, note taker, communicator, idea person, and so forth. Groups should meet at least twice a month and create a plan of action for their committee. To make teacher supervision easier, have all the groups meet at the same time.

5. Make a commitment to this type of student council for at least a year.

Discussion
1. Why should everyone be given the opportunity to be a leader?
2. Why is it difficult to make decisions in large groups?
3. How can we all become better decision makers?

Enrichment   Encourage students to join committees outside of school. Perhaps they can attend parent-teacher meetings, become more involved in their local YMCA or YWCA, or join sports or religious groups. Ask students to share their leadership roles and responsibilities outside of school.

Leadership Contract

By reading and signing this leadership contract, I hereby agree to live up to those standards required of all student council members:

1. I will act responsibly and exhibit qualities of good citizenship so I can serve as a positive role model for other students.

2. I will keep an open mind and listen closely to other students' ideas and opinions.

3. I will be accepting of all students, regardless of gender, race, color, creed, academic standing, extracurricular achievement, or popularity.

4. I will attend all student council meetings unless I am unavailable because of illness, family or school obligations, or emergencies.

Date: _____ Name: _____

What Do I Stand For?

Leaders must be able to verbalize what they stand for. This is often a difficult task for students. It is much easier for them to follow the group decision and not stand alone on an issue. This activity challenges students to think about what they stand for.

Materials ▶ Writing and art supplies

Instructions 1. Tell students that they are going to create their own personal creeds and mottoes. Have students first think about what they stand for. (This will be difficult for many students, so you may have to ask them to think about three rules to live by or three virtues that are very important to them.)

2. Tell students to develop their own personal mottoes or words to live by. Two popular choices are "carpe diem" and "try your best."

3. Have students artistically represent their motto and what they stand for. Some students may choose to do collages; others may choose to draw or use photos.

4. After the projects are completed, allow students time to share their works of art.

Discussion 1. Why is it important to know what you stand for?

2. Have you ever been in a situation where you had to compromise your values? What did you do?

3. How can you be true to your motto?

Enrichment Give students the opportunity to take a personality or self-awareness test to help them better understand themselves and their leadership styles. Various tests are available on the Internet.

| ACTIVITY 6 | Listen Closely |

Listening skills often seem to be forgotten by the time students enter middle school. Many students are easily distracted and have difficulty tuning in to what is being said. Teachers should continually help students develop their listening skills.

Materials
- ▶ 1 or 2 short stories
- ▶ Writing paper and pencils or pens

Instructions

1. Read a short story to your class in which numbers or colors are mentioned.

2. After you have read the story, ask the students to take out a sheet of paper and a pencil or a pen and answer some questions. The students who have listened closely will know which numbers or colors are mentioned in the story.

3. Have those students who do not pass this listening quiz take another listening quiz in order to improve their skills.

4. After you complete the activity, ask the students who were successful to share the secrets of their good listening.

Discussion

1. What distractions get in your way when you try to listen?

2. What helps you concentrate?

3. How can we become better listeners?

Enrichment

Introduce your students to the world of observation. Ask them to sit somewhere and quietly observe their surroundings: What do they hear, see, and smell? What do they observe that is unusual? Ask students to write a short essay about their experiences.

Post a variety of pictures around the room. Give your students 5 minutes to examine the pictures. Turn the pictures over and ask the students a series of questions pertaining to the pictures. This activity will help test and improve your students' powers of observation.

ACTIVITY 7   Planning

Another leadership skill that students need to develop is the ability to plan. Although many leaders like to jump in feet first, this is not always possible. Some leadership and decision-making opportunities do require thought and planning ahead of time. This is a fun activity that requires students to develop a plan before they begin.

Materials   ▶ Popsicle sticks and glue

Instructions

1. At the outset of this activity, have students work in pairs; remain hopeful, however, that they will eventually want to work together as a class. Inform them that they have been hired to build houses for a new development. Once completed, the development should house 20 families of all different sizes. Tell the students they have a limited amount of materials available to them and must complete their houses with the materials they have.

2. Give each pair the same number of Popsicle sticks and tell the students they must now plan their housing development. (It is at this point that you should hint to students that they might consider combining materials so they can develop a plan as an entire class.)

3. Encourage students to plan the design of their development, what features they want to include, and, if there are leftover Popsicle sticks, what else they can build.

4. Once plans have been completed, let students build their developments.

Discussion

1. What was difficult about this activity?

2. What decisions did you have to make?

3. What would you do differently next time?

Enrichment   Invite a city planner to your classroom. Ask him or her to discuss a city planner's responsibilities and also to bring in pictures of projects and anything else that illustrates the process of planning. What do city planners have to consider? What types of decisions do they need to make?

ACTIVITY 8   The Art of Working Together

Leaders need to learn how to work together and even how to follow. All groups and organizations depend on people who can listen attentively, accept and follow directions, and help implement a course of action. This activity encourages students to work together and take turns being the leader.

Materials
- ► Empty boxes
- ► Wrapping paper
- ► Tape and scissors

Instructions
1. Pair up students and give each pair an empty box, wrapping paper, scissors, and tape.
2. Have the pairs work together to wrap the package, but permit each student to use only his or her nondominant hand in the process. Thus each student will be using only one hand—the weaker hand—to help wrap the package.
3. Remind students that, in order to complete this activity successfully, they must work together and listen attentively.

Discussion
1. What did you have to do in order to be successful at this activity?
2. Why is it sometimes difficult working with other people?
3. Why is it important to have followers as well as leaders?

Enrichment
Students always have fun with the following activity: Once again, pair up students. Find a wide-open space appropriate for a three-legged race. Before the race can be run, the two students must stand as close together as possible so that the right leg of the student on the left and the left leg of the student on the right can be tied together. The students must then try to race as one to the finish line. In order to finish the race, the students will have to talk to each other and work together.

Challenge Activities for Leadership and Responsibility

For Students
- ► Have students take on leadership roles in your school. If none exist, find a way to create them.

- ► Have students get involved in an issue that concerns them, such as attending meetings, writing letters, or letting other people know about the issue.

- ► Encourage students to practice their public speaking. Have them start out by speaking in front of close friends or family and then help them seek out opportunities to speak to a wider audience.

For Teachers
- ► Accept the responsibility for a leadership role at your school. Join a committee and make your work meaningful.

- ► Create genuine leadership opportunities for your students. Let students make their own mistakes; hope that they learn from them.

- ► Get involved in a community issue that concerns you. Rather than simply discussing them with neighbors, teachers, and friends, help do something positive.

CHAPTER EIGHT

CONFIDENCE to TAKE ACTION

CONFIDENCE to TAKE ACTION

LEADERSHIP and RESPONSIBILITY

SPIRIT of ADVENTURE

CURIOSITY and CREATIVITY

FUN and EXCITEMENT

SENSE of ACCOMPLISHMENT

HEROES

BELONGING

ACTIVITY 1   My Portfolio

Students who are self-confident recognize and celebrate the skills they have. They are proud of their accomplishments. Students who are confident to take action do something positive with their confidence. They stand up for what they believe in and are willing to help others gain confidence.

Materials
- ▶ Folders
- ▶ Writing paper and pencils or pens

Instructions
1. At the beginning of the school year, inform your students that they are going to keep a portfolio of their work. Each portfolio will contain a variety of works from different subjects. Students will be allowed to pick and choose what they want to showcase.

2. Have students put at least 10 items in their portfolio each quarter. They should also develop a table of contents and a page that explains their rationale for including those items in their portfolio.

3. Make sure that each portfolio also contains a narrative written by you that highlights the progress each student has made over the quarter.

4. Allow the students to share their portfolios with their parents during open houses and parent-teacher conferences.

Discussion
1. What schoolwork are you most proud of this year? Why?
2. What subject have you improved the most in so far this year?
3. What subject could you help tutor other students in?

Enrichment
Ask for student helpers who are confident and competent in a specific area of study. The student helpers should designate several lunch periods a month during which they will help other students understand an assignment or get caught up on their schoolwork.

ACTIVITY 2   Parental Input

Parents obviously have a huge effect on their children's confidence. In order to help students develop their confidence, it is important for parents to be aware of their children's strengths and fears. This activity seeks the help of parents in developing their children's confidence.

Materials
▶ Student Input Form
▶ Parent Input Form
▶ Pencils or pens

Instructions
1. At the beginning of the school year, have your students fill out the Student Input Form and have their parents fill out the Parent Input Form. The object is simple: to complete each unfinished sentence. (Using this same format, feel free to add any other questions you would like to see answered.)

2. Be sure to tell parents not to ask their children for help in filling out the form. Let parents know that their children will eventually see the form.

3. Once you have collected all the forms, ask students to compare their answers with their parents' answers:

   How well do their parents know them?

   Did their parents' answers surprise them?

Discussion
1. How much alike or different are you from your parents?
2. When you are your parents' age, what do you think your greatest success will be?
3. If you could add another statement to the form that expresses another strength of yours, what would it be?

Enrichment
Invite parents into the classroom to share a bit of information about their careers. Their presentations should center on their setbacks as well as their successes. It is important for students to see that even adults suffer setbacks now and then.

Student Input Form

1. My greatest strengths are _____

_____.

2. What I like best about me is _____

_____.

3. My biggest fear at school is _____

_____.

4. I would like to learn about _____

_____.

5. My parent's biggest fear in school was _____

_____.

6. My parent's strongest subject in school was _____

_____.

Parent Input Form

1. My child's greatest strengths are _____

_____ .

2. What I like best about my child is _____

_____ .

3. My child's biggest fear at school is _____

_____ .

4. My child would like to learn about _____

_____ .

5. My biggest fear in school was _____

_____ .

6. My strongest subject in school was _____

_____ .

Raising Student Aspirations: Classroom Activities for Grades 6–8
© 2003 by Russell J. Quaglia and Kristine M. Fox. Champaign, IL: Research Press (800) 519-2707

ACTIVITY 3 — My Vision

Middle school students often don't take the time to think about their future and what they want it to look like. This activity challenges students to develop a vision of their remaining years of school, to envision—with their teachers' help—where they will be by the time they graduate from high school.

Materials
► Vision Sheet
► Pencils or pens

Instructions
1. Give students the Vision Sheet and have them complete it. Tell them to put in a great deal of thought before responding to each item on the list.
2. Collect the Vision Sheets, put them away, and give them to the next year's teachers. Ask those teachers to let the students revisit and revise their statements both at the beginning and at the end of the following school year.
3. Have the students revisit and revise their statements each year (completing the same thoughts, but on a brand-new Vision Sheet), all the way through high school.

Discussion
1. Why is it important to think about your future?
2. What dreams do you hold for yourself?
3. How can you make these dreams a reality?

Enrichment
Ask students to think about all the positive and negative qualities they have. For example, are they optimistic or pessimistic? Are they doers or procrastinators? Are they helpful or selfish? How will their qualities affect their vision?

Vision Sheet

Name: _____ Grade: _____ Date: _____

By the time I graduate from high school, I would like to

▶ achieve the following dreams: _____

_____

_____

▶ develop the following skills: _____

_____

_____

▶ overcome my fears of the following: _____

_____

_____

▶ be a better friend by doing the following: _____

_____

_____

The following people are those who can help me achieve my dreams:

_____

_____

_____

My pledge to myself is as follows: _____

_____

_____

_____

Raising Student Aspirations: Classroom Activities for Grades 6–8
© 2003 by Russell J. Quaglia and Kristine M. Fox. Champaign, IL: Research Press (800) 519-2707

Thinking on Your Feet

Students who enjoy the arts are often at a disadvantage if a school does not provide opportunities for artistic learning. Some students find their niche in math and science, whereas others blossom when they are exposed to music and drawing. This activity allows students who like to perform and be creative a chance to shine.

Materials ► None

Instructions 1. Have students form two lines that face each other. Tell them that they are going to put their acting and quick-thinking skills to the test by engaging in a dialogue with a student in the other line. (Have the first student in each line pair up to engage in a dialogue, then the second student in each line, and on and on.)

2. Set the scene yourself. For example, you might tell students that they are at the beach and a rainstorm is approaching. Feel free to change the scene midway through the activity.

3. Tell each pair of students that their task is to carry on a conversation relating to the scene you have set. Tell them also that they will face the following challenges as they converse with the student opposite them:

> The conversation must be carried out using questions only.

> The student who speaks first must begin with a question; the student who speaks second must respond with a question as well.

> The students continue in this manner until one of them fails to ask a question and instead uses a declarative sentence, or until one of them either repeats a question or cannot think of anything to ask.

> Students who blunder must sit down and defer to the next student in line.

4. Give the students several opportunities to perform this activity.

Discussion 1. What was it like to have to think so quickly?

2. What made some students better at this game than others?

3. What surprised you about one of your classmates?

Enrichment Another version of this activity can be used in foreign language class. Students should form one long line. The first student must say a word in the foreign language. The next person in line must think of a word that relates to the first word. For example, if someone says, "car," the next word uttered might be "fast" or "drive." You will notice that some students will be more comfortable and confident with their speaking skills than others.

ACTIVITY 5   Confidence Cards

Students need to hear words of encouragement every once in a while. Encouragement not only makes them feel good, it generally puts them in a good mood and helps boost their self-confidence. Students also need to know that someone believes in their abilities and has high expectations for them.

Materials
▶ Confidence Cards (created by you on the basis of your class's makeup) written on note cards
▶ A large bowl

Instructions
1. Put the Confidence Cards in a bowl. (Make sure you created enough cards so that each student can have two, if necessary.)

2. When students enter the classroom, ask them to close their eyes and choose a Confidence Card. The card will have written on it either words of encouragement (e.g., good luck on your test, you're great, the class enjoys your input) or instructions to complete a task (e.g., raise your hand in class, say hello to someone you don't know, help a classmate with homework). The activity continues as follows:

   If students draw a card that has words of encouragement written on it, challenge them to accept those words as a confidence booster.

   If students draw a card that asks them to complete a certain task, challenge them to complete the task so they can increase their self-confidence. (Tell students to replace their Confidence Cards as they leave the room at the end of class.)

3. Let students draw a card each day they enter your classroom. You will begin to notice that your students look forward to drawing their Confidence Card. As the year progresses, let students add their own cards to the bowl.

Discussion
1. What does it feel like to receive words of encouragement?
2. Whom do you encourage on a daily basis?
3. Why is it important to have a positive outlook?

Enrichment
Ask students to create their own Confidence Cards. Have them hand the cards out to their friends, teachers, or people they pass in the hall.

Friendship and peer opinions are always important issues in middle school. Students rely on their friends to help build their confidence and identity. This activity is a fun way for students to see how others view them.

Materials   ▶ Writing paper and pencils or pens

Instructions   1. Inform students that they are going to have a challenging task. They are going to think about how their best friend would describe them.

2. Have students write a short poem about how their best friend would describe them. The only catch is that the poem must be written only in similes. (Some examples: "She is as bright as the sun" or "She dresses like a pretty flower" or "She is as sharp as a tack.")

3. Allow students plenty of time to write their stories and share them with the class.

Discussion   1. What makes someone a good friend?

2. How can you be a better friend?

3. What is special about your best friend?

Enrichment   Ask students to create scrapbooks for a friend or a family member. Encourage them to include stories, pictures, and memorabilia in their scrapbooks. This project may take a bit of time—possibly several months—to complete.

Confidence to take action means confident students doing something with their skills. Confident students who do nothing are not helping themselves or others. This activity encourages students to think about taking action for a cause they believe in.

Materials
► Writing paper and pencils or pens
► Optional: videotaping equipment

Instructions
1. Divide students into groups of four and tell them that they are going to create a TV commercial. The intent of the commercial, however, will not be to sell a product but rather to sell an idea.

2. Have students think about a cause that is important to them. Next, have them think of ways they can help the cause or interest other people in the cause. All the while, students should be thinking of ways to develop a commercial that will garner support for their cause.

3. Have the groups act out their commercials for the entire class. If possible, videotape and show the commercials in this way.

Discussion
1. Why is it important to get involved in causes you believe in?
2. What one cause do you feel passionate about?
3. How can you make a difference for your cause?

Enrichment
Encourage students to get involved in a cause they believe in. Help students write letters to the appropriate people, those who also have an interest in the cause.

Many students have strong feelings about issues or concerns outside of school. Students should be encouraged, however, to use their energy and passion to help the school community as well. This activity encourages students to gather opinions and ideas from their classmates.

Materials   ▶ Writing paper and pencils or pens

Instructions

1. Let your students know that they are going to undertake a project that involves their interviewing other students at school.

2. Have the class work together to develop a list of interview questions intended to evoke student ideas and opinions about the school.

3. Have students practice their interviewing skills in class before they actually conduct their interviews.

4. Ask each student to interview five students. Make sure that students from all grade levels are interviewed and that these students represent a wide range of personalities.

5. Ask students to write summary reports of their findings.

6. Have students present their findings to the school's administrators.

Discussion

1. Why is it important to get involved in school issues?

2. How else can we gather student ideas and input?

3. What surprised you about the student input?

Enrichment   Ask students to interview their parents or siblings about a school-related issue. Have them analyze their responses. Do all the parents think the same? Is there a particular issue that needs attention?

Have students share their findings with school administrators.

Challenge Activities for Confidence to Take Action

For Students
- ▶ Encourage students to do something they are a bit scared of doing because they might not succeed. The activity should be challenging but safe.
- ▶ Ask students to share their skills and knowledge with their classmates or younger students. Have them offer to help with reading or math assignments, depending on their strengths.
- ▶ Encourage students to take the time to compliment at least one different student each day.

For Teachers
- ▶ Invite a colleague into your classroom to offer constructive criticism about a new lesson you are teaching.
- ▶ Teach your colleagues about something you learned at a workshop.
- ▶ Take the time to congratulate yourself on everything you have done this year. Recognize your successes.

About the Authors

Russell J. Quaglia, Ed.D., is the executive director of the Global Institute for Student Aspirations at Endicott College in Beverly, Massachusetts, and a professor of education. During an appearance on NBC TV's *Today Show,* he was described as America's foremost authority on the development and achievement of student aspirations.

A dynamic speaker, Dr. Quaglia travels extensively, presenting research-based information on student aspirations and motivation to audiences throughout the United States and around the world.

His opinions and comments on aspirations and controversial educational topics have been much sought after and published in national media such as the *Washington Post, Boston Globe, New York Times, USA Today, Chronicle of Higher Education,* and *Education Week.* He also has appeared on CNN and C-SPAN.

He received his bachelor's degree from Assumption College in Worcester, Massachusetts; a master of arts degree in economics from Boston College; and a master of education and doctorate from Columbia University, specializing in the area of organizational theory and behavior. Dr. Quaglia's research has been published in numerous professional journals, including *Research in Rural Education, Educational Administration Quarterly, Journal of Instructional Psychology, American School Board Journal, Adolescence,* and *Journal of Psychological and Educational Measurement.* His thoughts and opinions have also appeared in popular magazines such as *Reader's Digest, Better Homes and Gardens, Parent and Family,* and *Ladies' Home Journal.*

Kristine M. Fox is the director of field services for the Global Institute for Student Aspirations and an instructor at Endicott College. Most of her work involves teaching the importance of student aspirations to administrators, teachers, and students in schools throughout North America and abroad. In addition to working with these groups, she discusses with parents and other community members the significance of student aspirations.

She has presented extensively at conferences and workshops. She has conducted her site work throughout New England and also at a number of disparate locales such as Alaska, Arizona, Mexico, Toronto, and England.

She received her bachelor's degree from the University of Michigan and a master's degree in education from Harvard University. She has experience both as a classroom teacher and as a school administrator.